Fuck

Crap

Calm as
Fuck

Clusterfuck

Cock

Cumwipe

Cunt

Assgoblin

Love

Bollocks

Fuck You

Calm
your
balls

Cocknose

Hell

Cuntpuddle

Moron

Dickweed!

Dickweed

Fuckity
fuck

Damn

Fucknugget

Darn

Fuckstick

Fucktrumpet

Douche

Dick

Goddamn

Holy Shit

Independent

Dumbass

Audace

Fuckwit

Motherfucker

Nutsack

Piss

Pisswizard

Shit

Slut

Son of
a bitch

Twat

CPSIA information can be obtained
at www.ICGtesting.com
Printed in the USA
BVHW01s2044040418
512059BV00025BA/207/P

9 781945 260001